TABLE OF CONTENTS

CHAPTER 1 - CREDENTIALS

If I told you who I am you would be astounded. Let's just say I'm a very famous celebrity. For the purposes of this writing I'll refer to myself as Mr. Wayne.

Although I have never been much of a conspiracy theorist, opting rather for a zealous Christian faith expecting the Lord Himself to enact justice, I can in good conscience no longer remain silent.

At risk of sounding cliché, the names and situations have been changed to protect the innocent and the guilty, for that matter. Over the past decade the situation I am describing has gotten completely out of hand, and has become an epidemic in America, if not worldwide. My family has been threatened, conspired against, misled, harassed, and lied to repeatedly by three major banks, two title companies, a city, a county, a tax board, a builder, a realtor, a homeowners association, and three of its management companies. Even respected attorneys who wished to assist in combating this fraud by taking my family's case were scared off by the powers that be with threats of future career stagnation.

Given the wide and varied regular access that I have to the media, it is high time that I stop playing nice with the dog.

It all began in 1994 when after an aspiring career as a professional football player was cut short by injuries and multiple surgeries, I thought I'd do the responsible thing and complete graduate school. I'd always been a fine student having graduated tenth in my class of over 400 students at the local catholic, all boys, college prep school where I starred as a student-athlete. I went on to double major at a catholic university, again starring as a scholar-shipped student- athlete, captain of my team, and member of the exclusive scholars program which comprised only twelve students on the entire campus.

After graduation I pursued my dream of playing professional football until surgeries on both shoulders and double hernia surgery ended my ability to compete at the professional level. With a broken heart I begrudgingly trotted off to another fine catholic institution of higher learning to obtain an MBA. I again excelled in the classroom, taking classes part-time at night and on weekends while working in the corporate headquarters of an international fitness equipment manufacturer as Human Resources Manager.

It took me three long years to achieve my diploma, but again I received high honors for my scholastic excellence and was offered a scholarship to pursue a law degree from that same institution. Having had enough of school by that point I respectfully declined their gracious invitation and accepted a position as Director of a Fortune 500 consumer products company in another state; Hardly anticipating how valuable that law degree would have been. I was promoted to Vice-President and relocated to another territory in the western United States.

After barely getting settled in my new job I began receiving recruiting calls from all sorts of companies and even government agencies. The CIA, FBI, Secret Service, DEA, and Border Patrol all came calling. I might have been interested because I found the work intriguing and exciting, however the salary at a G-14 I recall they referred to it as didn't even cover my mortgage. At that point I realized a career as a government agent wasn't in the cards for me.

The other Fortune 500 positions I was being recruited for, however, did pique my interest as they were equipped with hefty salaries, large signing bonuses, even larger yearly bonuses, stock options and stock purchase plans. The corner offices were prime. The total compensation packages I was being offered were in no uncertain terms "the whole Magilla".

After being offered VP position at several major companies, I chose a Wall Street financial institution as the victor for my services. It was later revealed to me that my former company was a major recruiting target because of its reputation for employing the best and the brightest, and its world-renowned corporate culture and change initiatives. I was, in fact, at the top of every recruiters' and companies' list – the prize candidate or golden boy as they put it. My new company sent out some movers to pack up my shit and back east I went.

Upon arriving on the east coast I was immediately placed in ritzy corporate housing at 76th and Park Avenue. A corporate housing executive began working with me to find a six acre wooded plot outside the city where I could build my dream home. After eighteen months of construction and construction delays, I finally moved in.

All seemed well during this period. I truly was the golden boy, being wined and dined by the corporate muckety mucks, as well as being invited to the most secretive strategy meetings and political events. I was even asked to mentor employees in the exclusive management training program to assist in the development of more "ME's" – leaders for the future of the organization.

CHAPTER 2 - SUBTLE ATTROCITIES

In about 1997 or 1998 looking back at it, the first glimpses of disillusionment began. There were little things at first. Practices that didn't seem kosher, employees that didn't seem to be treated fairly, customers that were being lied to and actually discouraged from doing business with my company. These one-offs as I filed them into my conscience I merely chalked up to "it's just business".

In the beginning of my tenure I kept my mouth shut. After all who was I? Just the new guy. I thought to myself "what the hell do I know?" These people have been working here much longer than I had. I just kept going to work and trying to fit in. The more high level meetings I went to the worse it got. I walked around with a pit in my stomach, almost a feeling of disbelief with what I was hearing and privy to in these meetings. I began to speak up in disagreement and had many "talking to" by my boss about being a team player and just going with the flow. In my heart I knew what the company and its executives were doing was wrong, and there are just certain things that gnaw at a man more than the thought of political suicide. My friends said I was brave. My parents called me crazy, but after all they were the ones who instilled my Christian values in me in the first place so I defiantly resisted many organizational injustices.

As time went on, the atrocities grew. In one meeting an exec in marketing proposed that we begin to send out fake car payment coupon books before the real coupon payment books could arrive from the true finance company. The scam would work if the unsuspecting recipient actually made a payment to us. He called it "course of performance". We would in essence be taking over the note if someone would be foolish enough to send us the payment. The kicker to this scheme was when the group decided to target consumers who were age fifty-five and older because "people in that age group are more likely to just pay any bill they receive in the mail." This particularly rubbed me the wrong way because my honest, hardworking parents were well over fifty-five at the time. Of course I blew a gasket.

About this same time tensions were very high at the company because a proposed merger was on the table. Anyone with any corporate experience clearly understands that with mergers comes downsizing. The stress to impress ran at an all-time high. Stock prices soared. Everyone got rich and of course no one wanted to get laid off. Some employees were willing to accept reassignment within the organization, but nobody wanted to be shut out entirely.

Again, because of my position as VP, I was included in more executive level secret meetings to determine the new organizational structure. After moving thousands upon thousands of employees around in anticipation of the merger, the real work began after the merger was completed and announced to the public. Let's just say that's when the craziness began. The shit hit the fan so to speak. Rounds and rounds and rounds of organizational chart tweaking in meetings that waned long into the night ensued. I flew all over the east coast for at least three months gathering data for the inevitable reduction in force – the term that struck fear into the hearts of everyone but me. By this time I was actually hoping to be reduced because I was completely appalled and ashamed of the antics and actions of everyone I worked with. Their job was no longer to do their job. Their new job was to not get fired at any cost, even the cost of their own integrity and down-right deceit and collusion against customer and fellow employee alike. Corporate politics had seen its finest day. Greed was most certainly good in the words of Michael Douglass.

When I returned to corporate from my lengthy travels I uncovered more espionage. In the decisive meetings to reorganize the new company, thereby assimilating two huge organizations into one, further age discrimination was not only accepted but encouraged. Anyone over the age of fifty had a target on them and the company was actually very blunt about it. At the same time the operational segment of the organization had declared a witch hunt to rid us once and for all of what the company deemed "dead beat customers".

We actually set about a strategy to provide such terrible customer service to our customers who had medium to low net worth that they would become angry and take their business elsewhere. In essence, unless you were a customer that was deemed worthy of our attention, it was virtually impossible for you to transact business of any kind with us. We closed locations and outsourced all customer service in an attempt to frustrate all but the cream of the crop. In the organization's mind, why should we devote any time, attention or resources to anyone who wasn't wealthy? I refer to this phenomena as a Wall Street caste system or financial apartheid.

CHAPTER 3 - WHOLESALE DEFAULT OF THE AMERICAN LANDOWNER

It had always been my understanding through the ramblings of the media, every banker and every politician that I had ever read or heard, that banks hated foreclosing homes because they had no interest in holding property. They attempted to make the general public believe this myth by brainwashing everyone into thinking that these foreclosed properties were unprofitable and quite simply a diversion from the actual business of the bank. Banks simply had no use for homes or land.

I say hogwash! Does that make any sense? The central tenet of this country of ours is the American Dream. The most important component of said American Dream is home ownership. The founding fathers in their infinite wisdom put great emphasis on white, male landowners. Remove the white and the male circa 2012 A.D. and that leaves the rest of us seeking to be homeowners. This single goal drives everything we do, every decision we make and everything we believe in as Americans.

During my final days on Wall Street, considering the backdrop of organizational espionage, fraud, shady practices, discriminatory behavior, general paranoia and its resultant illegal decision making, I faced the final straw head-on. Approximately two months before my eventual exit, I attended a meeting with high ranking members of the mortgage business who were attempting to convince me to leave the retail division opting to work with them.

I had already decided to leave the company at that point, but I politely listened to their proposal since I had not informed my boss of my planned departure as yet. The conversation in that conference room got very interesting when I was relayed the mortgage businesses strategy to foreclose homes, take the property over for virtually nothing, and then re-sell said properties to high net worth clients in the Private Bank. The plan was simply a rich get richer while the poor get poorer typical scenario. What I'd suspected all along had just been confirmed.

Banks actually enjoy foreclosure because it gives them the opportunity to quadruple dip. In the infancy of a new mortgage, when the original homeowner makes his monthly payments, the bank profits from the interest on the loan. When they later seize the home after default by the mortgagee the bank collects insurance on the unpaid mortgage contract and owns the home. Lastly, they sell the house at a tidy profit and the whole fiasco begins again for the new owner.

This certainly doesn't sound like the terrible deal for the banks that they would lead us to believe. They publicly state that they would much prefer us to simply make our payments, but in most cases they collect from homeowners over thirty years.   If we default instead it doesn't require a rocket scientist to calculate the windfall profit from the quadruple dip and it doesn't take thirty years to recoup. All this certainly exceeds the original amount that the bank loaned the person in the first place.

After I digested all this information from my colleagues, I politely but firmly said thanks but no thanks and proceeded to apply for a voluntary separation package. I took my vested stock, my options, and two years of severance pay, later sold my home and left all the malfeasance behind – or so I thought.

CHAPTER 4 - CHANGE YOUR LIFE

Sickened to the core by everything I had just witnessed over the last two and one-half years, and being compelled to quit my job by what I now recognize as Divine Inspiration, I ventured out into Manhattan with a new career in mind.

By this time I was nearly thirty years old, but being tall, dark, and handsome, smart, talented and in great shape I pounded down the doors of six of the largest talent agencies in New York City. They in turn promptly slammed six doors in my face telling me I was at least ten years too late. The reasons for these rejections were numerous. I was too old, too muscular, and even too good looking! I didn't even walk correctly. Just before giving up for good I stepped into a rinky dink agency that no one had ever heard of, and probably had never gotten anyone any real work. It was the type of agency that everyone is warned about.

The kind that makes a living selling test photo shoots to unsuspecting hopefuls only to reject them later. Except that isn't what happened to me. The lady took a look at my only picture, read my admittedly weak resume, and exclaimed "you can play football"? I said "yeah, I'm damn good at it". She proceeded to tell me about a SAG movie that needed players and ironically the casting, actually a tryout, was that very weekend at some park in Weehawken, New Jersey. Of course I earned the part and the rest is history. I've been a famous celebrity ever since.

With my newfound success or Divinely Inspired luck I truly believed that I had put all the nonsense that took place on Wall Street behind me. I tried to block it out, not even thinking about it again. I figured wrong. Not so fast young man. The real story was yet to begin, and my experience on Wall Street turned out to be what made me ultimately realize that the conspiracy my family innocently and naively stumbled into could actually take place. As it stands today, had I not had my integrity bubble burst by the corporate machine, I wouldn't have been savvy enough to believe that the events that would transpire almost a decade later could have unfolded anywhere but in a Mel Gibson or Russell Crowe movie.

My family, who were the actual victims, was reticent to believe in conspiracy theories, and remain disillusioned and confused to this day. Their

American Dream has been shattered, turned into a nightmare really, amid aggressive attacks by banks, builders, title companies, the IRS, cities, counties, tax boards, and a clueless homeowners association who have all conspired and colluded to steal their home rather than admit their mistake as they all got caught with their hands in the proverbial cookie jar. Reminiscent of the Enron debacle, and unfortunately, what has become increasingly common with the Kenneth Lay and Bernie Madoffs of the world, the most amazing series of cover-ups, lies, collusion, and heinous deceit, including bully tactics are regularly substituted for an admission of guilt, a fessing up, or even a simple apology.

In this case my 80+ year old parents were targeted as the victims, leaving me with no other alternative but to expose this unfortunate situation to you the reader and the American public. I must use my position as a media darling and my experience with the unethical and illegal practices of the mortgage industry to prevent this from ever happening again to any American. This has now become my life's mission.

CHAPTER 5 - YOU CAN'T CHEAT AN HONEST MAN

Father Wayne was a Cowboy in Northern Michigan in the 1940s when FDR's New Deal was instituted across America. The history books herald FDR and his policies and programs as integral to the success of America. Father Wayne has a different and strangely surreal perspective. His personal experience with the New Deal is not only tragic, but eerily similar to the conspiracy surrounding his home today.

I was brought up with my dad spouting American pie adages like you can't cheat an honest man and your word is your bond. It didn't take me long to realize he was kidding himself, my mom and me in the process. I'd always appreciated his honest, wholesome outlook. My father never, ever lied or took anything that didn't belong to him. To this day he is still the most honest and hardworking man I have ever known or even heard of for that matter. All the more honorable is that he maintained his integrity despite how the New Deal was really the Raw Deal for him.

Father Wayne grew up on his ranch with his elderly and sickly grandparents. His mother dumped him off with her parents and fled to the big city with her new husband after the man who impregnated her, grandfather Wayne deserted grandmother Wayne when she was but three months pregnant. Father Wayne's grandparents raised him on that ranch from day one and were the only family he ever knew until grandfather Wayne resurfaced when he was well into his twenties. As the health of his grandparents deteriorated, father Wayne ran the ranch full-time from nine years of age. When he turned eighteen both grandparents had passed on and the ranch was his.

During World War II FDR would send his agents out to the ranch to ensure that my father was working since farmers and ranchers were typically left to produce for the nation rather than to fight in the war. After WWII ended, some idiot came up with the concept of the New Deal. As it applied to father Wayne it went down something like this: Some government men confronted him on his ranch spouting good news about farm subsidies and the like. My dad's ranch was only eighty acres and he worked like a dog just to feed himself and his cattle. The Raw Deal he received limited the land he could grow crops on to an untenable amount, and of course the subsidy was grossly insufficient. Even more despicably, father Wayne was forced to reduce his already miniscule herd of cattle.

The worst part was that he wasn't allowed to butcher or sell his cattle at market. Instead, while FDR's men looked on, father Wayne shot his cattle and burned their carcasses. On a plot of land that measly, father Wayne had just shot and burned his way into bankruptcy. The New Deal- what a bunch of crap! Knowing that he couldn't survive under the new conditions, my dad sold his remaining equipment, farm implements, the remainder of his cattle and his ranch to his uncle who owned the adjoining larger farm and could make ends meet. It was off to the big city for father Wayne. By the time I was born he'd been driving a truck for twenty years. As soon as I was old enough to understand, I realized how the Raw Deal had shattered my father's soul, how much he loved the country, how much he detested city life, and how none of us should have even been there in the first place. I marveled as he never missed one single day of work, never took one nap, rose every day before sunrise, and the only time I ever saw him lay down except to sleep at night was when he had an excruciatingly painful kidney stone. When it was time to go to work, however, he rose from the dead and took off in his truck. He's still the toughest son-of-a-bitch I know.

My father finally retired a few years after I left home. My mother retired a few years after I left Wall Street. At advanced ages in their seventies and eighties, as my dad is ten years older than my mom, I finally felt that they could rest from their many labors. My only solace, given that neither of them was very healthy, was that they could live out their remaining years in peace. What transpired next as my parents searched for their retirement home transformed that anticipated peace into a living hell.

CHAPTER 6 - A SIMPLE PURCHASE

In late 2004 while living in Miami, I received a call from father Wayne saying he was going to California to look at some homes that he and my mom could live the rest of their lives in. The cold weather was apparently killing them in their current residence. Since I was managing the family trust, he wanted me to know what he was planning from a financial standpoint.

After looking at several properties my dad decided upon a home that was currently under construction. It was a 1.37 acre lot that backed up to an undevelopable mountain. After negotiating with the builder, Gary, and the builder's sales person, Maria, my dad offered 1.4 million dollars for his dream retirement home. My dad returned to his house, told my mother about the purchase and excitedly called me. I then flew from Miami to California to work out all the specifics with Maria.

When I met with her to sign all the contracts on behalf of the family trust, everything went smoothly and nothing seemed amiss. Maria walked me around the property, confirmed the size of the lot as 1.37 acres, and told me the house would be ready for my parents to take possession. I did notice another home under construction next to my Dad's house, but I was assured by Maria that everything was in perfect order. She procured a mortgage broker that she insisted my dad utilize. As she put it, "they had a great relationship and had done business with that company throughout the rest of the neighborhood." Maria also insisted upon the title company my dad was to use stating that they were also very familiar with the builder and worked closely with this particular mortgage company. I wrote a check for the deposit and went back to Miami.

The house wasn't completed on time, but that is typical with new construction I surmised from my personal experience in having several of my own homes built. My parents actually took possession of the home in May 2012. Prior to taking possession, my parents drove to California and completed a final walkthrough with Gary. The house next door was now nearly complete and appeared closer to my Dad's house than it was originally presented to him on the map Gary used to sell him during my dad's initial visit. That map would eventually turn out to be the key to a vicious bait and switch scheme that prompted this entire account.

Gary swore up and down that my dad in fact had received his full 1.37 acres. Skeptical, my dad called his attorney who contacted the title and mortgage companies who also swore up and down that his property line was accurate and his title was free and clear. With those assurances my dad signed off and began to make arrangements to move into the home.

CHAPTER 7 - I GOTTA MOVE THE FENCE

As part of the compliance with the guidelines established by the homeowner's association, father Wayne was required to submit his landscaping plan to the association's management company and to the city's approval department within ninety days of his purchase of the home. In about July 2005 my parents had not yet moved, but I was shooting in California and offered to assist my dad with his landscaping plan. I contacted a local architect to design the pool, Jacuzzi, fire pit and landscaping required in the front and back yards. I received the plan back a few weeks later detailing a 250,000.00 dollar construction project. I walked two copies of the plans into the management company and they assured me they would send one copy to the appropriate person at the city for approval. The plan cost my parents $3500.00.

I stayed at the house for the duration of my shoot and bought my parents some drapes, furniture and décor from a local decorator as a housewarming present. One day my agent was at the home with me discussing an endorsement deal when the doorbell rang. I found that odd due to the secluded location of the home and the fact that hardly anyone knew I was staying there, but I answered the front door and to my surprise Gary, the builder was standing there.

I had never met Gary before, having only dealt with Maria, but he introduced himself and I invited him in. After the typical small talk and celebrity gazing, Gary proceeded to confide in me that he was having extreme difficulty selling the house next door. Although he listed it at 1.3 million dollars, a 100,000.00 dollar reduction from the price of my dad's house, he said he couldn't sell it because everyone was complaining that the back yard was too small. His solution to that problem was to move the rear wall next door back fifteen feet. To accomplish this he said he needed to cut into the hill and put in a new drainage system.

Things got murky when he said he wanted my dad's approval to move my dad's rear wall that was adjoining the current wall next door because the homeowners association insisted that the walls line up to ensure uniformity in the neighborhood. I knew damn well my dad would never go for it, especially since I had just turned is his landscaping plan with his current yard dimensions. I knew my dad would never consent to paying another 3000.00 dollars for a revised landscaping plan. Gary insisted so I called the old man and put him on speakerphone with me, Gary and my unsuspecting agent. In typical cowboy fashion my dad told Gary to shit on a wooden rock, and yelled at me as usual for even considering such bullshit. My agent got a laugh and Gary went away dejectedly. A few weeks later, back to Miami I went.

CHAPTER 8 - THE LONE NEIGHBOR

I was comfortably back in Miami, my parents were making arrangements to sell their home and began selling some of their possessions at garage sales. In December 2005 I was required to attend some business meetings in California so I decided to stay at the Wayne residence to keep an eye on the place and conduct my meetings there.

When I arrived at the house I was greeted by a somewhat frantic neighbor named Summer. She lived next door to the vacant house next to my dad's, and with photos in hand proceeded to tell me that Gary had not only moved the wall next door, he actually moved my dad's wall further back and replaced the drainage system behind it. Holy shit, I knew father Wayne would be furious. I'd never seen it go very well for anyone who disobeyed him and he'd given Gary a very clear order to buzz off.

Summer followed me into the house as I carried in my bags and sure enough a new wall, fifteen feet further back was now erected in my dad's yard. Talk about trespassing! Armed with Summer's pictures of the bulldozer in dad's yard I left an angry message on the builder's answering machine demanding an explanation. I knew father Wayne wouldn't be pleased about paying for a corrected landscaping plan. I thanked Summer and walked her out. I called my dad and my intuition from thirty-eight years of experience with him was correct. My ears are still ringing from the verbal barrage of an old cowboy.

It took almost ten months of leaving messages for Gary and almost everyone else at his construction company before I got a response. In the meantime tragedy struck the Wayne family. As my parents were nearly ready to move into their dream home, I got a call in Miami one rainy afternoon that I will never forget. Father Wayne who had heart bypass surgery a decade earlier was in failing health and needed to remain home for a myriad of tests, doctor visits, treatments and extensive medication. To make matters worse, my mother was in need of two knee replacements and two hip replacements. Due to their medical needs they both decided to remain where they were familiar and comfortable with their physicians.

CHAPTER 9 - THE INEPT HOMEOWNERS ASSOCIATION

In mid-2006 I still had not heard back from Gary so I took it upon myself to get some answers regarding the movement of the Wayne wall without father Wayne's approval. I made a special trip to Los Angeles on a private jet to attend a meeting of the neighborhood homeowner's association to complain. To my surprise they had absolutely no knowledge of the wall caper and actually attempted to bully me into having father Wayne sign some lot line adjustment papers and pay two-hundred dollars which was their fee for moving the fence. When I objected a very tall two-hundred and fifty pound man tried to intimidate me raising his voice and actually shoving me. Not being one to be intimidated I stood my ground and told him to stick his fee and his lot adjustment paperwork up his ass.

This was the first incident in which I suspected collusion might be in order, yet I had no proof and left the meeting with more questions than answers. This association is a stickler for even a weed in a homeowner's yard. Residents are required to seek their approval to do almost anything. I found it hard to believe that Gary performed a major construction project right under their collective noses without any sort of approval, if not from the association, at the very least obtaining city approval. After all why would the association be upset with the Wayne's? We didn't move the wall, and furthermore, we objected vehemently to its displacement altogether. I should have given them a bill for the three thousand dollars I would have to pay the architect to revise the already submitted landscaping plan.

When 2007 rolled in I finally heard from Gary. He and his associate David met me at Wayne Manor after yet another special trip on my part. They apparently recognized that they could no longer duck the Wayne's since they had converted the house next door in to a sales office for some townhomes they were building in the area. I didn't mince any words with either of them regarding their ill-advised movement of the wall. In response I received a flurry of psychobabble about a misunderstanding. Anyone who has ever encountered a displeased father Wayne knows very well that there was no possibility of misunderstanding. Besides, my agent and I heard the entire conversation. I heard excuse after excuse about how the yard next door was too small to sell the property and how Gary was losing his ass. Gary and David further remarked that they were having a dispute with the other owner of their company, Pat, and proceeded to blame him for the entire mess. Of course they denied any culpability for the conduct of the association. I agreed to their invitation for a lunch meeting the next day to sort out the matter.

I brought my agent to the meeting because I didn't want any more misunderstandings. To my chagrin, about two minutes into the luncheon, Gary asked me if I wished to purchase the house next door. I looked at my agent and laughed. My response was what the hell is on your mind man? Are you on drugs? You move my dad's fence unilaterally after the house was sold, and you think I'm going to bail you out of your small yard problem? I stood up to leave and Gary blurted out I'll sell it to you for nine hundred thousand dollars because Pat and I are suing each other. I stepped outside and conferred with my agent, a very shrewd business man and former Wall Street trader. He advised me to have the property inspected before I immediately said no. I went back into the restaurant and informed Gary that I would consider it if they agreed that I could have the home independently inspected. Gary and David conceded. My agent pulled up in his BMW and we sped away.

It took me a few months to schedule and meet an inspector because I had business to attend to in Miami. When I finally got back to California and the home was inspected, I was informed that the home had several structural issues including an uncompleted attic and studs that were too far apart. My decision to decline was easy to arrive at with this new information having been disclosed.

I told David who at this point was actually living and working in the home that the Wayne's had no interest in purchasing their property. I also informed them that father Wayne was considering legal action over the wall scandal and that Gary should get it sorted out with the city and the association. Again, back to Miami.

CHAPTER 10 - MALFEASANCE AT THE MANAGEMENT COMPANY

Around the same time as my meeting with Gary and David, I spoke to a man in the neighborhood named Scott. Actually, Scott and his friend Todd recognized me driving through the neighborhood and followed me up my father's long, winding driveway trapping me in the garage. My agent was in the house reviewing a script from a movie I was considering. Scott and Todd barged their way into the living room, both of them tipping the scales at over three hundred pounds.

I was thinking at that point that I was going to be forced to defend us. Then Scott and Todd started yucking it up like a couple of awestruck assholes asking me if they could come to the Oscars with me as my bodyguards. Fools are everywhere in California and these two were no exception to the rule. After more small talk and general nonsense Scott proceeded to tell us that he was running for a board member position at the association because the previous management company had been terminated for malfeasance. That was no shock to me given the horrible treatment I had received at the association meeting.

In over two years since I delivered my dad's landscaping plan to the association and the city, father Wayne had never heard back regarding approval to begin the construction projects. We merely surmised that the approvers were busy with the other one hundred ninety plus homes in the neighborhood, and those homeowners had purchased their homes long before we ever showed up. That's when the letter came from the new management company claiming that my father was negligent and assessed him a fine for failure to submit his plan.

To the next association meeting I went with the plans. Yet again the board members accused us of failing to submit the plans even though the people I had submitted them to were fired for malfeasance. Typically, my plea fell on deaf ears and I was accosted about the lot- line again. At that point I left the meeting before I got pushed around again. The next day I delivered two more copies of the plan to the new management company. One copy was for them and the other copy was yet again for the city planning person. I was promised that the plans would be reviewed and father Wayne would be apprised of their decision. At this point the homeowners association continued to pile on fines to father Waynes monthly maintenance fee for failure to landscape his yard on time. The plot thickens! Of course father Wayne refused to be extorted by incompetents. He knew we submitted the plans well ahead of schedule. To date the fines are over seven thousand dollars and counting.

CHAPTER 11 - FORCED TO REFINANCE

In my first meeting with Maria she was adamant that my parents must do business with the builders' title and mortgage companies. After my father received a call from the mortgage company I further suspected that something fishy was going on. I just couldn't wrap my head around what the motive was. Father Wayne was informed via telephone by a representative from his mortgage company that there was a minor discrepancy pertaining to his title. This problem could only be cleared up, according to the representative, if my father refinanced his home. Furthermore, he would be required to put another one hundred thousand dollars down in order to refinance. What a racket! The mortgage company was unwilling to disclose the specifics about the title problem, explaining only to us that the title was not free and clear as the title company had claimed. My father complied and informed me of the new payment amount as I had been paying the monthly mortgage from the Wayne family trust. Shortly thereafter my dad was stricken with cancer and began a series of fifty-two radiation treatments.

After the refinance my father and I contacted the mortgage company on several occasions inquiring about the new free and clear title we were promised. On multiple occasions we were told that the mortgage company was expecting the title company to provide it to us very shortly. The quintessential check's in the mail scenario. This charade played out until one day my father received written notification that his mortgage company had been purchased by another bank. Father Wayne now had a new bank that was certainly willing to collect his money, but there was no recognition by said bank as to where the hell our new title was.

Next, I finally heard back from the city about the landscaping plan. A woman from the city planning office called me to notify me that the plan was denied, citing trees that were flammable, drains that were missing and trees that were too close to the house. I paid yet another architect two thousand dollars to adjust the plan that included the expanded back yard created by Gary's lies.

Yet another homeowners association management company had bitten the dust. This second company didn't last long and was summarily dismissed for malfeasance just like the first management firm. Therefore, I, on behalf of the Waynes, resubmitted the new landscaping plan to the new management company and in turn to the city for the third time. It didn't take long this time until my dad called me furious while I was on the beach in Miami that they denied his plan again for minor bullshit. Father Wayne, completely disgusted with the incompetence of the association and the city took matters into his own hands. Sick as a dog he flew to California and went to his home to resolve all this nonsense, or so he thought. Upon arriving in California my dad noticed that many of the homes in the neighborhood had signs in their yards from the same landscaping company. Aha! He imagined. He proceeded to call that company and a woman named Sue met him at his home. She indeed had built all the pools and satisfactorily completed, per city requirements, many landscapes in the area. She measured the yard, whipped up a plan taking into account all the feedback the city had provided with their denials of previous plans, and promised my father that she would personally deliver the newest plan to the city where she had a fine relationship with the woman who determines the approvals. This only cost my dad another twenty-five hundred dollars much to his dismay. My dad, upset, yet hopeful got on a plane and went home for his radiation treatment.

I again flew to California a week later after Sue had completed her finishing touches on the plan and met with her at the house for final approval. It looked fine to me and Sue confidently jumped in her truck and headed to the city planning office. She returned to Wayne Manor an hour later with a man she introduced to me as her partner. I expected them to tell me we were all set at last. Denied. Sue went on to tell me some of the craziest shit I had ever heard. She explained to me that she indeed walked the plan into her friend's office at the city planning board. Her friend examined the plan and denied it to Sue's amazement. She was told that the dimensions of Wayne Manor were not consistent with the dimensions the builder had filed with the city and the county tax board to gain initial approval to develop the lots in the first place. Sue angrily went on to relay to me the rest of the conversation. Sue's contact at the city proceeded to give Sue the same lot line adjustment papers that the homeowners association had attempted to force my father to sign. The woman who denied the plan communicated to Sue that if she could get father Wayne to sign the lot- line adjustment and pay the filing fee that she would expedite the approval of Sue's plan. Sue and her partner stormed off yelling that they had measured the dimensions themselves and that they were indeed correct.

Both Sue and her partner advised me to instruct father Wayne to again refuse to sign the documents and remarked that this situation was a cover-up of the highest order. They added that the city planning person had known this all along and had been smokescreening us with the petty reasons for previous plan denials. I thanked them for the information and their honesty and never saw them again. Stunned I walked back into the house and sadly called father Wayne. He was too sick to even get mad. I now knew for certain that this was a circle-jerk, even third parties like Sue recognized a cover-up when they were confronted with one of this magnitude. I was immediately worried about my parents' health, knowing that their retirement dream was certainly a nightmare they couldn't resolve in their condition. Even with all my experience surrounding illegal business practices, lies, deceit, politics and malfeasance gained from my stint on Wall Street, I was clearly out of my league. I would soon discover how far out of my league I really was.

CHAPTER 12 - THE LETTER

Dear Mr. Wayne: This is your mortgage company. Apparently your former lender, which we purchased, made some serious errors in your initial loan and the subsequent refinance of that mortgage. Please contact blah blah blah at blah blah blah. The above was a letter received by father Wayne in 2008.

I didn't know about the letter until I went to visit my Dad after one of his more grueling cancer treatments. Sitting in his kitchen, flanked by my mom and dad, I hesitantly dialed the number. Considering the current barrel of monkeys, I could only imagine in my wildest nightmares the can of worms I was just an 800 number away from opening. I was right.

After my initial call and thirty more like it comprised of hour after hour after hour after transfer after dropped call and starting all over again, I never did get to the bottom of the admitted mistake. Another cover-up of confusion that my former employer would have been proud of was unraveling in front of my eyes. I now believe that the bank was attempting to get us to commit suicide from our collective frustration. With seemingly no other recourse I just stopped calling them.

CHAPTER 13 - SUMMER'S OVERHEAD PHOTO

After a few weeks in Miami I had to return to California for a thirty-six day shoot. By now I was dreading my stays at Wayne Manor and they were seriously distracting to my career, my life and even my health. As usual, here came Summer to greet me from down the road. Her appearance typically brought bad news. We exchanged niceties at which point she produced a photo from her purse. It was an overhead photo of Wayne Manor and the house next to it. At first I couldn't believe what I was looking at. After careful examination, I realized so many things all at once that I nearly had a panic attack.

First of all, Summer's photo clearly showed Wayne Manor's property line running through the middle of the house next door, through the backyard and behind the wall that Gary moved. The initial suspicions of father Wayne when he was completing his walkthrough in late 2004 were now confirmed. The litany of subterfuge by the city, the association, the builder, the mortgage company and the title company had just been exposed by an old adage – a picture's worth a thousand words or excuses in this case. My father was wrong all along.

You actually can cheat an honest man. My father paid for 1.37 acres. The builder, bank and title company confirmed that he received 1.37 acres. The tax board based his county property tax on 1.37 acres. But what everyone involved in the cover-up knew, including the woman at the city, was that my father only really received one acre. That's why the dimensions didn't match. That's why he couldn't landscape his yard unless he wanted to violate a city ordinance. I wanted to vomit because in the words of Old Testament Job, what I feared most had come upon me. The Wayne's were indeed victims of the very sort of foul play that led me to leave a lucrative career on Wall Street a decade earlier.

I emotionally hugged Summer who said she discovered the photo on the internet while doing some research on her own property. I thanked her repeatedly for being such a wonderful neighbor. She went home and a billion thoughts ran through my brain. On one hand I was relieved because I finally knew what had been going on. The Wayne's, including me, had been lied to, avoided, and misled for so long because the powers that be were all in cahoots, clearly protecting the developer as well as their own greedy interests. Summer had caught them all with their hands in the cookie jar. I wondered how many payoffs had changed hands. After all, how could every inspector that ever came to this construction site ignore a lot line encroachment of over one-third of an acre?

Mostly I felt bad for my parents who were in a 1.4million dollar battle with city hall for virtually all of their retirement money. The mortgage company certainly knew or why the mysterious refinance due to a title problem or the vague letter from the new bank which unwittingly purchased the problem in their acquisition of the famously fraudulent and predatory lender? How could I learn my lines? All I could think about was now what? I considered selling the home but by now it was no longer worth 1.4million. The value had fallen below nine hundred thousand dollars, and without a free and clear title it wouldn't be ethical to sell Wayne Manor, thereby dumping the problem onto some other unsuspecting person – probably somebody else's parents. I couldn't stomach that and I knew father Wayne had too much integrity to even discuss it with him. I did vomit. Then I didn't get much sleep.

CHAPTER 14 - DAVID COMES CLEAN

Prior to my father's purchase of Wayne Manor, Gary and David had been using the converted two-car garage as a sales office. They left behind some interesting artifacts in the vacated office space. The most fascinating was an illegal electrical utility box hidden behind a secret mirrored closet. The box was designed to by-pass the regular electric meter which was located outside. When I first discovered the bogus wiring I contacted the police. To my surprise they were not at all interested and advised me to contact the electric company. The electric company accepted my call, but shockingly they were not interested either.

I'd been stewing about the illegal utility box for a few months since I discovered it and the secret closet. Now, however, after Summer provided me with the incriminating photo I couldn't tolerate even one more iota of bullshit. I walked next door where Dave was living and working, and confronted him while he was kicking a soccer ball off a gate that accessed a private service road to the city water tower behind Wayne property. Dave turned white as a ghost when I showed him the photo. It wasn't but two seconds before he started singing like a bird. David turned into the king of all stool pigeons. I'd finally gotten the confession that the Waynes were due all along.

David began to spin an elaborate tale of lies, deceit, conspiracy and dastardly deeds that even I hadn't suspected. Dave's version went like this: When Gary and Pat turned in their development plan to the city and county for approval of the 190+ homes to be built in the sub-division, Wayne Manor, Dave's home/office and Summer's home were the last to be completed and sold. After construction of the Wayne home had begun and after my father's purchase was finalized in December 2004, Gary had just barely broken ground on the house next door. Summer's home was already completed and she was about to move in.

Dave's home, however, had a significant problem. A service road that was to run along Summer's property bordering Dave's property was installed by the city in the wrong location. The road was to be used only by the city to access the water tower located directly behind Wayne Manor. The city goofed when it positioned the road to bisect Dave's property in half.

This left Gary with insufficient room on either side of the road to build the home in question.

Faced with the option of foregoing a 1.4 million dollar property, or instead undertaking an arduous if not completely impossible adjustment to the plan they'd submitted for official approval, Gary decided to build the home on the Wayne property without telling anyone. Afterward Gary bribed the city and county officials, as well as the mortgage and title companies to turn a blind eye to his fraud. Furthermore, Dave stated that Gary intended to file a bogus lot line adjustment when he moved the walls in question. When father Wayne objected, Gary panicked and forged my signature on the documents. The dubious plan went awry according to Dave when an employee of the county who was in the dark with respect to the entire conspiracy, suspected foul play since Gary attempted to file the application for lot - line adjustment many months after father Wayne had closed on the house. The low level county employee also noticed that the signature was not my father's but mine that Gary forged which had no authority since the house was my dad's and didn't belong to me. To this very day said application remains unapproved. Gary ignored that minor detail and moved the walls when no one was looking - or so he thought. Summer came to the rescue with her photos of a CAT bulldozer in the Wayne yard and the wall under re-construction.

The entire caper finally made perfect sense. The cover-up was exposed by an overhead photo and a complete confession. I now recognized my only course of action. Since the new mortgage company had no involvement in the original scam perpetrated by many including the previous mortgage company, I decided to give them one more opportunity to assist father Wayne in seeking justice. My prior experience with them after the letter fiasco didn't deter me. I created a detailed package of the facts and again sought to contact the bank, but this time I would do it in person thereby avoiding the infinite loop of telephone avoidance. Father Wayne is not a litigious man, and to this point had held off suing the builder for the wall caper, so I determined to extend one last Christian olive branch to settle the matter.

I flew back to Miami after my shoot wrapped and began to prepare all the data including Summer's photos for the Bank. After all, they sent my dad a sincere admission that their predecessor had screwed up. They would certainly see these facts and admissions as irrefutable. I was completely confident that they could get father Wayne's land back and a free and clear title. Besides, as the holder of the note, the bank had a vested interest in accuracy and justice. I have never been more naive in my assessment of any situation.

Before I contacted the bank I made a call to Simon, an attorney friend of mine in California. I inquired what legal options would be available if in fact the bank played dumb. Simon told me that if he took the case he would seek complete demolishment of Wayne manor and Dave's home. Then he would insist that Wayne Manor be built in the proper position per the original city-approved map. He proceeded to state that he would then sue the title company for all father Wayne's money back. Next, the tax board would be sued for taxes paid on the .37 acres that were not received by father Wayne.

Lastly he would sue the city and the homeowners association for collusion. The mortgage company would be sued separately for conspiracy, and predatory lending practices against the elderly in the original loan and unnecessary but forced refinance including fraud with respect to the additional down payment and failure to resolve the title as promised. WOW! What a complete disaster. I knew Simon would win, he made perfect sense and the evidence strongly supported his position. In the end I decided to enlist the bank's assistance one last time to avoid all these proposed court proceedings. My parents were in failing health and I had incomparable career expectations placed upon me by agents and studios. I didn't have the luxury of devoting any more precious time to policing the world of bank and construction fraud.

CHAPTER 15 - HOW DID THEY SELL THE HOUSE NEXT DOOR?

It was the first quarter of 2008 by the time I put all my evidence into a format that I thought the bank could decipher and understand. My dad was nearing the end of his radiation treatments and my mom was getting to the point where hip replacements were her only option to maintain mobility and minimize horrific pain. She could never have climbed the grand, winding staircase at Wayne Manor. I took the private jet back to California to visit the sprawling banking complex that the new bank had acquired in its purchase of the old bank.

As I drove up to the Wayne home I was shocked to see a party rocking Dave's house. Even more disturbing was my phone call to Summer to ascertain what the hell was going on and who were all these people on father Wayne's .37 acre. Summer said Dave had taken off like a bat out of hell after I left town, and Gary dumped the property for less than eight hundred thousand dollars to a real estate investor who in turn rented it to some drug dealers.

Summer was considering moving because the exclusive property that she fell in love with because it provided a safe haven for her daughter had turned into an enclave for misfits speeding up the hill in the middle of the night buying weed and cocaine and disturbing the peace. My initial thought was how in the hell did they sell that property without a free and clear title? If my dad didn't have a proper title then they couldn't possibly have one either.

Apparently this town didn't conform to the laws the rest of the country followed. I nearly expected Wyatt Earp to come walking up the driveway. This truly was a time-warp back to the wild wild west. Upon further investigation I noticed that both the front and back yards were now completely landscaped. Again, how in the hell could they get city permission to landscape if father Wayne couldn't? If Wayne Manor's dimensions were off by .37 acres, then applying sound geometric principles, Dave's old sales office must be off by the same .37 acres when compared to the original map on file at the city and county tax board. Were their title company and mortgage company now co-conspirators as well? Someone had a lot of explaining to do. Sue's comment about a conspiracy of the highest order seemed all the more appropriate in light of these latest developments.

The house was jumpin', the music was blarin' all sorts of characters of ill repute were smokin' weed and snortin' coke right out in the open on the front balcony. Naked women were runnin' all around the backyard smokin' marijuana and drunk. I went to the gym to escape the frat party ruckus and when I returned I tried to get some sleep to no avail as the party continued until at least the next afternoon. In the morning I got up, showered and gathered my evidence file. Off to the Bank with me. Party on neighbors.

A few months later, with the party still raging on next door, a police officer knocked on the front door of Wayne Manor at nine p.m. one evening. In the cul-de-sac there were six squad cars, three unmarked cars, and a DEA van. The officer informed me that an apparent domestic squabble had escalated and when the cops arrived on the scene they discovered a house and garage full of marijuana plants and other drugs. The officer asked me what I might know about the situation. I let him know that I typically lived in Miami and was only there that week for a business meeting. Satisfied, the officer excused himself and everyone went to jail. The next time I came to California, Dave's old house was vacant, Summer was ecstatic, and the big wig investor had allowed the house to go into foreclosure. Was order restored? I thought. Not even close. What the real estate investor attempted to do to me in 2009 is more unbelievable than anything I have ever read in all the movie scripts in my entire acting career.

CHAPTER 16 - I STORM THE CAMPUS

I drove up to the large bank campus, walked into the building and stated my case to some guy at the front desk. He immediately informed me that I was at the wrong location. He then gave me directions to another large campus across town. I again parked and walked in, feeling a bit redundant I spoke to the guard at the front desk. Quite rudely he told me that if I wasn't making a mortgage payment that no one would see me.

I explained to him that I had flown all the way from Miami to inform the bank of a seriously fraudulent matter. The guard didn't care and told me to leave. I politely told the guard that I wasn't going anywhere until someone in authority at the bank listened to what I had to say and accepted the file I had prepared with all the data I had collected over the last three years. He phoned someone in the legal department and instructed me to have a seat in the lobby. After about forty-five minutes, four ladies came out to greet me with great trepidation. They treated me like a terrorist at the airport, nervous and shifty. They escorted me to a back area with a few chairs and inquired as to what was on my mind.

I communicated to them the details of father Wayne's unbelievable situation. Like nuns they pretended to be very sympathetic. One actually divulged a story about something similar that had happened to her elderly father. After looking at Summer's map they took me into another back conference room. A woman named Yvonne and two of her cronies joined us in the conference room a few minutes later. Yvonne accepted my file and told me that the bank would investigate the matter and get back to me. I thanked the group of ladies, took Yvonne's phone number and drove back to Wayne Manor. Off to the private jet and back to Miami.

CHAPTER 17 - WHAT DOES A LOAN MODIFICATION HAVE TO DO WITH MY TITLE?

Yvonne called me within a week. I was laying out on South Beach with some topless models when my phone rang. Yvonne told me that she and some employees from the legal and policy departments had reviewed my file. The group decided that father Wayne's situation could be resolved by simply calling a woman named Ruth in the Hope Department. Yvonne gave me Ruth's number and told me the lot- line, title and previous mortgage companies mistakes would be rectified very soon. Great, I exclaimed!

Just the response I had been seeking since the conspiracy slowly unraveled piece by piece over the last three years. Finally, I thought, someone who gets it! My part-time detective work and previous experience with bank illegalities and cover-ups had made a dent in the armor of collective fingerpointing, lies, and failure to accept responsibility that made the Keystone Cops look entirely competent.

I walked home to my condo and dialed Ruth. As her phone rang I thought to myself, what a stupid name – the Hope Department was. I wasn't hoping for anything. In the words of Simon, there's another house on my property – get it off! Ruth answered. I explained the situation again like a broken record and told her that Yvonne had instructed me to deal with her to resolve the matter and hold the conspirators accountable. Ruth replied that she would ask me thirteen questions and then determine if father Wayne was eligible for a government instituted loan modification.

I said OK, but why would he need a loan modification to resolve a title and border dispute along with the banks admitted improper loan processing by their predecessor? Ruth assured me that this was the bank's method of handling such problems. After answering her questions and after an hour on hold, Ruth transferred me to someone else who informed me that father Wayne had indeed qualified. The gentleman then informed me that father Wayne would be receiving via fedex something called a workout package that should be filled out and returned. Oddly, the man also stated that father Wayne should discontinue making his usual mortgage payment and would soon begin paying eight hundred six dollars per month instead. None of this sounded accurate to me, but I didn't work at the bank so I had to take their word for it and respect their procedures and government program.

I immediately called Yvonne and left a message expressing my concerns as to how this course of action would resolve the matter at hand. The next afternoon Yvonne returned my call and said the workout package would explain everything clearly and the bank's legal department would begin chasing down the title company for the new title father Wayne had been promised when he refinanced.

I had a ton of work scheduled in California so I decided to stay at Wayne Manor for an indefinite period. When Ruth and Yvonne's workout package didn't arrive when they said it would, I again called Yvonne. She informed me that the bank, because of volume, was running six months behind on delivering workout packages to customers. After she said that I understood why I got nowhere when responding to their original letter. Obviously their predecessor had defrauded many more people than just my father, and the news on TV and in the papers each day confirmed this fact. Half the country was suing the previous institution for predatory mortgages.

Yvonne then stated that she would have someone from the Hope Department contact father Wayne to instruct him what to do until the workout package could be sent out. I explained to Yvonne that I paid the mortgage out of the family trust which I managed. She then told me to begin paying eight hundred six dollars instead of my usual payment each month and to merely send it in with my mortgage coupon, crossing out the usual amount and handwriting $806.00.

A few days later I got a call from father Wayne and he wasn't happy. My dad said someone from the bank called him and instructed him to write something called a hardship letter that was required for his situation to be resolved. When my dad told the man that he didn't have a hardship, the man asked my dad to get some paper and dictated the requisite information to my dad. The man then told father Wayne where he should mail the letter since my father did not have a computer or a fax machine. My dad sent me the letter and I in turn faxed it in for him.

As months went by and the workout package never came, I continued making monthly payments of eight hundred six dollars per month. Each month my dad was contacted by the bank and dictated another hardship letter that we faxed in. Additionally, the bank demanded that he provide information about his monthly expenses and my parent's income and assets. I called Yvonne to find out what the hell was all this about, and yet again she insisted that this was the process.

I then told Yvonne in no uncertain terms that this was ridiculous and my dad was a proud man and was very uncomfortable with having hardship letters dictated to him. I also told her that my parents had been on social security for over fifteen years, and I would not have them being badgered each month for financial information when their income hadn't changed in that entire time. She gave me some B.S. and I told her she better get this resolved immediately or the bank would be hearing from Simon.

Apparently she wasn't cooperating as she pretended to be. The Waynes never heard from the same bank employee twice, and whoever contacted us had no clue as to what was going on, preferring instead to psychobabble us to death. Frustrated, my father wrote a letter to President Obama informing him of how the bank was abusing the President's government program that he had no need of personally in the first place. He detailed the lies in each hardship letter that the bank was dictating to him.

After that father Wayne began receiving letters from the bank to be patient that they were addressing his concerns. I am certain that the bank was not on the up and up and was merely delaying the matter. What the bank didn't know is that I would eventually garner inside information regarding their practices. Two of my former Wall Street colleagues I would come to find now worked in their legal and policy departments. Yvonne and her team of liars wouldn't be fooling us for very much longer. My friends inside the bank would make certain of that. One of those insiders was much closer to me than the bank could ever have imagined. Let's just say I knew her biblically.

CHAPTER 18 - COLLECTIONS CALLS

An interesting development took place after I made two months worth of eight hundred six dollar payments. Unbelievably father Wayne began receiving collections calls from the bank. Everyday a new person called to inform him that his payments were delinquent. No shit father Wayne would respond to each day's multiple callers. Yvonne and her Hope Department told me to stop paying the mortgage to resolve the fraud I reported! Some of the callers even tried to convince my dad that the Hope Department didn't even exist! Talk about underhanded tactics. This daily barrage of calls went on for at least two years. Father Wayne was beside himself. A sick man should not have to deal with such nonsense.

Of course I called Yvonne who tried to convince me that these collections calls were perfectly normal and the situation would be resolved when the workout package arrived. Of course the package never, ever, did get delivered. Yvonne and the bank were not dealing in good faith. I attempted to persuade them that they should be going after the builder and the rest of the conspirators on the Waynes behalf since their predecessor was duped along with my father into granting a mortgage on a property that was not the size or location it was presented to be by the parties in question.

I started personally returning father Waynes calls to the would-be collectors. I was wasting an average of five hours per day for over six months, and father Wayne was doing the same. Now we were both getting collections calls! I even had several callers tell me that there was no hope department as they had attempted to convince my father. More lies! Two different individuals actually tried to convince me that father Wayne didn't qualify for the program that Ruth put him on in the first place. To appease their stupidity and persistence I actually answered the same thirteen questions again and then they said that NOW he was qualified. This was utter nonsense and red tape like I had never even heard of. I am a smart, educated , experienced and successful man. Every employee of the bank was a fool.

My career had taken a back seat to dealing with daily subterfuge on the part of over two-hundred different bank employees. Each day another person wanted to begin at square one rather than the point to which Yvonne said we had already progressed. The entire ordeal was maddening. I couldn't waste any more time with this, nor could I allow the bank to continue the torture of my elderly parents who were merely following every course of action prescribed by the bank no matter how nonsensical. Unfortunately, this matter would never be resolved according to the bank's approach. I was left no other recourse but to retain an attorney for father Wayne.

CHAPTER 19 - THE SHAKEDOWN GOES AWRY

The twists and turns in this incredible scenario were nothing if not entirely unpredictable. The man who purchased the home next door apparently wasn't as innocent as he appeared to be with respect to the marijuana growing fiasco. I'd never met the man but one afternoon when I answered the doorbell I immediately deduced his apparent involvement. A stout man intent on frightening me, shaking me down, or possibly killing me barged into my home.

He was ranting and raving about me blowing the whistle about the drug operation next door. I was not in the mood. I cut the man off in mid sentence, swept his feet out from under him and bounced him off his head on the hardwood floor. The look in my eyes must have sent a chill down his spine. I told him in my best former football player voice that I was going to tear his fucking head off if he didn't get the hell off my property immediately.

I also stressed that if I ever saw or heard from him or any of the assholes next door again that there was going to be an ass kicking of epic proportions. He must have gotten the message because when I yanked him to his feet and shoved him out the door by the scruff of his neck he silently left Wayne Manor without so much as a word. I'm sure in his line of work he'd never run up against someone of my athletic ability who could so easily mop the floor with the thug.

Months later while I was outside a theatre where a comedian friend of mine was performing, my cell phone rang. To my vast astonishment it was the dickhead real estate investor from the house next door. He told me who he was. That's as far as I let him get. I told him I knew he had put a hit out on me and I told him I'd better never see him or hear from him again or else. His response was that he would never do that. Apparently everyone in California takes me for a fool. I was having none of it. I hung up and have never heard from either of them since. I can assure you that I am no one to be trifled with.

And for the record: I didn't report the drug operation to the police. I had absolutely no idea that they were growing marijuana in that house. Summer told me they were dealing drugs, not growing them. As far as I was concerned they were just loud partiers. I don't stick my nose into other peoples' business. Period.

CHAPTER 20 - BANK EMPLOYEES ARE WELL TRAINED LIARS

Everyone at the bank had lost their minds. No organization could possibly be as incompetent as this bank was behaving. They were refusing to accept responsibility for the actions of their predecessor, and my friends in the legal and policy departments were about to make me aware of the bank's position regarding my property. They would soon divulge to me the following strategy: Delay, Delay, Delay, let the statute of limitations run out – and then foreclose the property.

Not yet knowing this simple fact, Yvonne kept telling me, and I believed her, that the workout package would arrive – SOMEDAY. The collectors increased their frequency and ferocity and there was no title resolution in sight. All the while the value of Wayne Manor had plummeted from 1.4million dollars to a market value of less than eight hundred thousand dollars. Father Wayne couldn't even sell the property without the corrected title, and the lot-line wasn't resolved either.

In all father Wayne was approved, and disapproved for the "government program" four times. Promises of the package, the new title, and the lot-line resolution were hollow, idle talk by now. I had to accept the fact that this bank was the same as the old bank, and exactly the same in its underhandedly blatant promotion of illegal and fraudulent activity as my former Wall Street employer.

The latest insult to my intelligence was when Yvonne told me that when the collectors hit us with their thrice daily calls that father Wayne and I were to tell them that she said we were waiting for a workout package and "paying $806.00 as we go."

CHAPTER 21 - GOTTA GET A LAWYER

Simon referred me to a colleague of his who specialized in dealing with lot-line disputes. Angel was her name and I was hoping that she would be. After reviewing the evidence I had compiled which had tripled since I began dealing with the Hopeless Department, now renamed to some other catchphrase, and filling a bankers box with all the apology letters the bank had sent us, Angel pronounced easy victory. How can anyone deny this overhead photo? She exclaimed!

After eighteen more months of eight hundred six dollar payments, no progress on any of the issues, and thousands of hours on hold, Angel never was able to coax the nebulous workout package from the bank executives. After a myriad of excuses by the innumerable bank idiots she dealt with, really all she was able to do was submit more dictated hardship letters from my dad and more monthly statements from my parents checking and savings accounts demonstrating that their income never fluctuated one red cent. More quicksand, more redundancy, more time and money wasted, and more stonewalling tactics from the bank.

Finally Angel called me one day and stated "If the bank refuses to deal in good faith and address any of these blatant and obvious offenses, failing for over two years to provide the workout package, I advise you that you have no other recourse than to discontinue making your $806.00 payments. How that bank can call it the Hope Department is beyond reason."

CHAPTER 22 - THE IRS

Another country heard from. In their infinite wisdom the IRS sent father Wayne a demand letter for California state income taxes due. Without any proof at all, they surmised that father Wayne could not have afforded to make the mortgage payments without taking in rental income from Wayne Manor. I wrote the IRS a letter explaining to them that indeed I had been paying the mortgage out of the Wayne family trust and that my parents filed state income tax in the home state they lived in for over fifty years. The home had never been rented to anyone ever!

As usual they refuted my claim and currently have an unjustified thirty thousand dollar lien on Wayne Manor. I'm almost certain that they are not co-conspirators as every other party in this case is. What I am certain of is that they are just a bunch of buffoons attempting to collect any money they can in a nearly bankrupt California. Why would I be surprised when the powers that be lay heavy burdens on people that don't deserve them, or in this case, are not even liable for taxes in that state? More nightmares for American Dreamers.

One side note to add: My dad called me last month and informed me that his perfect 800+ credit score has been sullied by this matter, and in fact his credit card company recently revoked his credit card. All this happened to a man who despite being summarily kicked off his farm, never failed to make a payment to anyone in his entire life until the bank advised him to stop paying them. America sucks.

CHAPTER 23 - EXPANSIVE SOILS

Normal daily functions such as going to the mailbox or answering the phone had become a comedy of errors. This day was no different and a new clown was about to announce his presence. As I got the stack out of the box I noticed a letter from an attorney named Joe.

> *Dear Mr. Wayne: I have been representing homeowners in your neighborhood who have been suing Gary and Pat's construction company. You see your entire neighborhood has been built using expansive soils which are not up to code. The homes in your neighborhood are experiencing serious damage due to the use of these inferior soils. Please contact my office at blah blah blah to discuss this matter further as I would like to represent your case as well. Sincerely, Joe.*

Against my better judgment, I called Joe, he met me at Wayne Manor and assessed all the cracks, stuck doors, dysfunctional garage doors, and excessive erosion of a backfilled hill and stated that Wayne Manor was one of the worst cases in the entire sub-division. Great I thought, more good news. Gary and Pat had screwed everyone with their illegal and shoddy business practices and now the entire development was going to sink to China.

I told Joe about all the other issues that Angel had dealt with and showed him Summer's map. He was amazed to say the least. He went on to tell me that Gary and Pat's attorneys were fighting him tooth and nail until the day of trial and then miraculously wanted to settle with him on the courthouse steps to avoid certain defeat.

He went on to say that he had developed a working relationship with their attorneys and that they were more than willing to settle each and every case with him rather than be exposed as scoundrels in front of a judge. He told me he'd draw up a contract to represent father Wayne and get back to me in a couple of days to begin the case. Unbelievable, I surmised – the Wayne's had stumbled into certain victory for once.

Amazingly, three days later I got a call from Joe informing me that he could not accept the case. I said you solicited me, I said yes, and then you turned down this one case in an entire neighborhood of professed easy victories? Joe, obviously embarrassed, told me that on the record he didn't think my home had enough damage.

A direct contradiction of his statement that Wayne Manor was the worst case he had ever seen. I said OK, what's the off the record reason for your decision. Joe confided in me that after speaking to Gary and Pat's attorneys they kindly let Joe know that if he wanted to continue his good relations with them and other influential attorneys, judges, city and county officials and had any hopes of any form of financial gain or career advancement, that he shouldn't touch my case with a ten foot pole. The conspiracy continued, and actually, had reached the highest level – OUR JUDICIAL SYSTEM!

CHAPTER 24 - THE MYSTERIOUS BANK MEDIATOR

Near the end of 2010 Angel was getting stymied, and Joe had been frightened off of a slam-dunk case. Once again I was forced to put my career on the back burner and take matters into my own hands. I called Yvonne and informed her that I had collected plenty of evidence to sue the bank, the builder, the title company, the city, the county tax board, the house next door's bank and their title company, and the homeowner's association for fraud. I explained to her that if I didn't get some answers fast that I would not hesitate to involve the press. After all, I have access to world-wide media and I wouldn't hesitate to spill the beans on every TV and radio show in America. My literary agent fully expects this book to end up in Oprah's book club due to its importance to the average American.

I must have gotten her attention because she transferred me to the legal department, who transferred me to the policy department, who sent me back to a higher level of the legal department, who sent me to the CFO, and back again to legal. After all this I was told that the reason that this matter was dragging on and on was because the bank was disputing my evidence. I couldn't believe what I just heard. I'm a very busy man. I didn't have time to play games such as making up an avalanche of evidence.

I had collected this evidence piece by piece over many years through eyewitness accounts. How could they possibly dispute it? And why would they bullshit me about some process when they didn't believe any of the evidence from day one? The bank went on to say that the only way to avoid a lengthy court battle would be to mediate the situation. They wanted me to terminate Angel and deal with their mediator, Harlon.

Harlon would survey the property, investigate my claims with the builder, city and county, and if he found my evidence to be legitimate then the bank would negotiate a settlement with the Waynes. I said fine. That sounds perfect for I knew that my evidence was spot on. Summer's photo and Dave's admission made me certain I knew what I was talking about.

Without informing me, however, that the bank was sending a local notary to father Wayne's home to get approval for Harlon to mediate, father Wayne turned the notary away at the door. Always cautious when strangers showed up at his door unannounced, he thought it was some sort of a scam. The bank called me to ask father Wayne to cooperate, and eventually he signed their approval paperwork.

In January 2011 the bank sent Harlon to meet with me at my home. I gave Harlon all the paperwork and details. He proceeded to do about a month's worth of due diligence, meeting with city officials, county officials, the property tax board, he tracked down Dave from next door, and more. His findings verified my evidence in each and every case. He actually uncovered details that I didn't even know about. Harlon wrote an extremely detailed report that explained the degree to which the builder failed to follow the plan he filed with the city and county. According to Harlon's research, not only was Wayne Manor encroached by Dave's old house, the builder had actually rotated the homes from their approved positions to face several degrees more to the north. He also found gross discrepancies in the original mortgage paperwork from the now defunct first mortgage company. There was no doubt that father Wayne did not get the property as it was promised to him in the mortgage contract and the title was clearly flawed.

Harlon presented his findings in a report to the bank and to father Wayne. After several months of conference calls with the bank it was determined that if father Wayne paid the remaining five hundred plus thousand dollars on the loan that he would own the home outright and the bank would ensure an accurate title from the title company.

Since Harlon was not a bank employee, but rather the mediator that they regularly worked with and assigned father Wayne, and since Wayne Manor was in a trust, the bank's CFO and legal department informed me that we would pay Harlon. Harlon would pay the bank, and then and only then would the bank transfer the deed to Harlon who would in turn transfer it to the Wayne trust. At last I thought the bank would make good on the promises of its predecessors from the refinance years earlier. The bank CFO told me that the title company had insurance for such situations and that they would owe father Wayne an amount potentially up to 1.4million dollars – the original price of the home.

That made sense to me because it agreed with Simon's statements years earlier. Father Wayne and I agreed that this solution would be acceptable and we could finally move on with our lives again rather than seek complete demolishment per Simon's counsel. Harlon and the CFO suggested that the bank of the house next door would in turn purchase the .37 acres from father Wayne at market value as well once OUR title company presented them with Harlon's report. I paid the money, Harlon filed all the paperwork the bank required, and the Waynes were thrilled that the matter was resolved. The yard could be turned into the beautiful landscape we had all envisioned. Not so fast, Wayne. Banks are crooked to the core and this one was brilliant in its scheming.

CHAPTER 25 - CONFERENCE CALLS AT THE HIGHEST LEVEL

While we were waiting for the bank and Harlon to complete the paperwork and get an amended title, I received a notice in the mail from Razzle mortgage. Razzle was claiming that Father Wayne's mortgage company had assigned the servicing of his loan to them. I called Harlon, he called Razzle, Razzle gave him the runaround which led to conference calls with Razzle, Harlon and me as participants. That led to more conference calls with Harlon, me and the real mortgage company. Again these led nowhere as the bank played dumb. Harlon fedexed the settlement package from the real bank to Razzle – that too was ignored. Now both me and father Wayne were receiving collections calls from Razzle.

More letters to the bank and to Razzle – we just paid five hundred plus thousand dollars and the nightmare was accelerating. The fraud was obviously contagious and expanding to new organizations. Justice was not being served and news stories about settlements with other homeowners pointed out that we weren't the only ones dealing with bank fraud.

CHAPTER 26 -WHERE'S MY TITLE?

After about another month of the shell game by both the bank and Razzle, accompanied by twice as many collections calls even though the note was entirely paid off, I implored Harlon to send Razzle a cease and desist notice on behalf of father Wayne. Razzle ignored the notification and kept right on bowling for dollars, literally driving the old man insane.

I jumped on the phone with Harlon and dialed the bank. We were bounced around again from department to department with everyone denying the truth about Razzle. Legal continued to tell us that everything was in process regarding the Wayne Manor title, and that they were in contact with the bank for Dave's old house to settle with them as the original mortgage company had promised during the ill – fated refinancing.

I knew they were full of shit, but Harlon stayed positive, assuring me that he had dealt with the bank before, and that although they were highly incompetent they always worked it out in the final analysis. That's why the bank involved him after all I supposed. They were so stupid they needed a third party mediator to do their work for them.

To date Wayne Manor's title is not worth the paper it is written on. Eight years of fraud and denials and counting.

CHAPTER 27 - DOUBLE CROSSED BY THE BANK

I contacted my bank insiders and explained what was now happening. I was informed that I was being double-crossed by the bank. They had taken the money from Harlon and the insurance from the mortgage, and had assigned the note to Razzle in order to foreclose on Wayne Manor.

Once foreclosed, they would have the house too and it would be nearly impossible for father Wayne to ever seek justice. In fact Razzle was now preparing to sell the note on Wayne Manor to yet another third party to further assist the bank in distancing itself from the crimes of its predecessor. In the process they threw father Wayne and their own third-party mediator under the bus.

CHAPTER 28 - TITLE CLAIM DENIED

After receiving Harlon's initial survey and report, I sent a copy of his findings to the title company and filed a title claim as I was instructed by the bank's legal team. When they received the package including Summer's now infamous photo, I was contacted via email and instructed to call a claims administrator. The woman I spoke to denied the claim and any responsibility as well as stating that I would have to supply more information if I wanted to appeal the decision.

The evidence I had already submitted was meticulously thorough and Harlon's interviews and admissions were indisputable. When Summer's map was taken into consideration, it was obvious that I was being blown-off. Certainly no more information could be required to prove that father Wayne's title was insufficient and the title company was definitely involved in the coverup. For God sakes the city wouldn't let him landscape. They indisputably knew that the .37 acres was encroached upon.

I explained to the administrator that their inspector was either negligent or "on the take" because he made a .37 acre oversight. This wasn't a few feet we were disputing. She unbelievably conveyed to me that the title company never even deployed an inspector to view the property. What an indictment! How can a title company charge you to verify a title if they won't get off their asses to do their due diligence? What a joke the home purchase process is. Exorbitant fees are charged for required assurances, but said assurances aren't worth a hill of beans! These procedures or lack thereof require serious reform and overhaul. President Obama needs a government program to pretend to deal with that too.

CHAPTER 29 - SMALL CLAIMS COURT

Next I got a notice in the mail that the Wayne Trust was being sued in small claims court by the homeowners associations' management company. I was actually excited to settle this matter once and for all, and brought all my documentation to court on the date supplied in the letter.

The case was delayed when I got to court because the association attempted to have the matter reviewed by a mediator instead of the judge. I was wise to this tactic and refused to have the matter heard unless a real judge presided. I knew that they had bribed that mediator because Scott from the association let me know ahead of time. When I went back to court on the rescheduled date a month later, the same situation was re-enacted. The association wanted to have the matter determined by the part-time judge who really wasn't a judge at all. Again, they had bribed that official as well according to Scott. I again refused to have the matter heard and was forced to wait until the very last case of the long day had been decided by the real judge in another courtroom.

The management company was attempting to collect some seven thousand dollars in bogus fines that it had levied against my father for what they called his failure to landscape his property. As if he wanted to have a 1.4million dollar home sitting there with dirt and dust blowing into it on a constant basis instead of the two hundred fifty thousand dollar beautiful landscape he had designed! The association was obviously foolish in pursuing the matter since the only reason that the yard was not landscaped was because the city wouldn't allow it.

Once the real judge sat on the bench the association representatives lost the case almost immediately when they lied to him about whether or not they knew about Summer's map and the city's denial of father Wayne's plan. The representative said no, and the judge pulled out a letter from the management company's attorney threatening the Wayne's if we did not landscape.

Also attached to that letter was Simon's response revealing everything that we knew at that time about the conspiracy to the association's attorney two years earlier. The judge responded by admonishing the association's representatives stating that "Mr. Wayne obviously has many more problems here than merely his failure to landscape."

Although the case was thrown out of court the incorrigible management company filed a judgment against father Wayne for the entire seven thousand dollars. That action begs the question – what the hell is the purpose of going to small claims court? The association obviously had to pursue this course of action or it would have been admitting its knowledge of and part in the broader conspiracy to defraud the Wayne's.

Another interesting comment made by the judge was that had father Wayne landscaped, it would have been in violation of a city ordinance. He continued further also stating that the investor who purchased Dave's old house had in fact landscaped in clear violation of that same city ordinance since his dimensions were skewed as well. No shit! Chalk one up for the Wayne's!

CHAPTER 30 - FOR SALE AGAIN!

A real estate company's for sale sign was posted at the mailbox of Dave's old house. They were once again attempting to sell that house without a free and clear title and while it sat squarely on Wayne property.

I contacted that real-estate company and spoke with one of the owners who met me at Dave's house the next day. I immediately invited him to Wayne Manor and handed him the same package that the bank, Razzle, the title company, the association and the small claims court judge had received. He didn't have to read very far before noticing Summer's map. He was shocked, stating he couldn't sell the property like this. I also informed him that I knew about the internet advertisement clearly displaying the entire lot line fiasco and seeking an all-cash deal for easy close. I also let him know that the inspection report I had received on that house detailed faulty construction that wasn't up to code, and furthermore, the expansive soils were not up to code either. I also stated that he and his client (the bank) were attempting to dump this problem off on another unsuspecting home buyer.

I have no idea how they were going to get around the title problem again. The city and county also knew what was up. They must have been turning a blind-eye to the matter or being bought off. As a good Christian, I extended yet another olive branch – this time to Charlie the broker. I offered him three hundred thousand for the property to his surprise. I told him that was my offer and to tell his bank that I would put the cash in a suitcase. I figured that must be the way everyone is used to dealing around here. Cash talks and mortgages walk. I also asked him to inform the bank that if they didn't accept my generous offer, I wanted them to kindly remove their home from Wayne land.

A few days later Charlie called me. I fully expected his and his bank's cooperation. Wrong again. Dejectedly Charlie informed me that his bank reviewed Harlon's report and Summer's overhead photo and boldly stated, "fuck him, we have an accurate title". For the first time ever a picture wasn't worth a thousand words and hence another bank refusing to deal in good faith. The trend is clearly nationwide with banks.

More trouble for the Waynes, I thought. Now we would be forced to sue the new neighbor, the realtor, the neighbor's bank and their title company as well. I wondered when, if ever, anyone would take responsibility for cheating my father. The Waynes were being persecuted and for everyone else it was merely business as usual.

The ironic part was that while their bank was in the process of showing the house next door, prospective buyers were trespassing all over Wayne property and even ringing my doorbell (one man just barged into my foyer without even knocking while I was in the shower) to inquire about the home. It seemed everyone knew there was a problem from the photos on redfin.com that illustrated Dave's house in the exact spot it sat, but showed the actual property to that house vacant, outlined in red, much closer to Summer's house, and on the other side of the service road. When I merely relayed the truth to these suckers that was detailed online for everyone to see – the bank had the nerve to send me a cease and desist letter. My response was how about you get your house off our property. That never deterred them and despite several unreturned calls to Charlie they sold the house anyway.

CHAPTER 31 - FORECLOSURE? YOU CAN'T BE SERIOUS

The next piece of mail I received at Wayne Manor was all the more ridiculous than anything that had come before. Even though the home was now paid off in the agreement between Harlon, the bank's self-appointed third party mediator, and the bank itself, Razzle now notified me of its intent to foreclose! In this manner they would put the final nail in the coffin and succeed in burying the cover-up for all the conspirators.

I made many calls to the bank and to Razzle, but none of them were returned. They were dealing in bad faith and they knew it so the best strategy was to avoid the Waynes. With an auction date set I could no longer fool around following all these prescribed solutions by the bank. They had just robbed me of five hundred thousand dollars and now they were after all of an eighty-seven year old man's net worth! I had to face reality. No one was ever going to admit to this conspiracy. My only recourse was to sue EVERYONE on behalf of the Wayne Trust. I knew that once I got to court any judge worth his robe would see what was going on. I needed someone as perceptive as Judge Judy or at least the judge in small claims court.

CHAPTER 32 - WAYNE STRIKES BACK

As a man of faith I determined that this entire situation must have been a test from above. More specifically I understood in my heart that I must stand on the side of right and use my position as a celebrity to shed light on this type of corruption that has affected so many Americans.

Ironically a note came to my door soliciting the exact assistance I was seeking. I called the number and a man named Constantine answered who after hearing my plight referred me to a real estate attorney appropriately and biblically named Noah.

I met with Noah who promptly began to sue everyone involved and soon began to be stonewalled in the mire of lies perpetrated by the bank and title company. The foreclosure was delayed by the judge who must have been familiar with complaints about bank practices. If you've turned on the TV in the past five years you couldn't help but understand that banking and mortgage fraud is a pandemic that even the President of the United States has been forced to address.

The bank attempted to blame Harlon for the entire mess, but they have two fatal flaws in their argument. One, the bank's conduct in addressing this matter was egregious and deceitful long before they introduced Harlon into the equation. Secondly, Harlon was their solution as mediator, endorsed by them, against father Wayne's will. Therefore, the bank's contention that he made mistakes falls squarely back on their shoulders. I refer to this as the but- for clause. But- for the bank's insistence, there would have been no Harlon. He was their resolution, not ours. Lastly, the evidence clearly spells out the conspiracy every step of the way, and there is no statute of limitations on fraud and cover-ups despite the bank's strategy to confuse us and waste our time until the clock had ticked away. A strategy that was divulged to me by the employees of the bank themselves.

I had no idea how to get to Noah's office as the address wouldn't register in my GPS. I drove on in the direction of the city his office resided in, and knew immediately that I was led to him by God. I merely followed a rainbow that ended right atop Noah's building. I was obviously destined, with Noah's assistance to bring this matter to the public and to battle it out in court to a bitter conclusion. God obviously needs someone like me, someone truthful and fearless to make a stand against the bank's intention to snatch homes away from hardworking Americans. I am proud to serve HIM.

CHAPTER 33 - THE MEDIA

Always reluctant to be an activist, I have done everything in my power to keep this matter private despite my public persona. I have many, many friends in the written, oral, and viewable media, and they are chomping at the bit to expose this story for what it is – clear evidence, that as I discovered during my tenure on Wall Street, that banks will resort to any measures to take homes from Americans insuring that the rich get richer at the expense of the poor. Banks seize property and sell it to the wealthy at pennies on the dollar. That is an undeniable fact. What could be more opposed to the American Dream?

Hence, I sit here and write this orderly account of the facts and details of the injustices heaped upon one of the last remnant true American heroes, father Wayne. A man who once again is in jeopardy of being summarily evicted from the land he bled to obtain.

I will be touring with this book and exposing this scandal in print, on TV, radio and the internet until father Wayne sees justice – once and for all. I will never give up.

The impact that my actions will have on the American banking system and economics as we view them will be severe. No longer will hardworking people be kept in the dark as to in whom they are placing their trust and their meager financial resources. Banking reform is long overdue and is necessitated by countless other injustices to a host of father Waynes.

CHAPTER 34 - IN GOD'S HANDS NOW

I know there is a God. His name is Jehovah, Jesus, and the Holy Ghost. He serves justice for all his children one way or another. As I eagerly await my deposition and day in court, I can only pray for Divine Intervention. Through God's Will the bank and its co-conspirators must be slain in a modern David meets Goliath story. How fitting that God Himself determine the outcome of the financial futures of a bevy of father Waynes across this land. It is in fact time for a New New Deal. A Deal that comes from the Hand of a Loving Father. In Christ Jesus. Amen. And all God's people said Amen and Amen.

THE END

9 798453 229956